zen-

FRANZ XAVER MOZART

POLONAISES FOR PIANO

6 Polonaises mélancoliques Op. 17,　4 Polonaises mélancoliques Op. 22,　2 Polonaises Op. 26

フランツ・クサヴァー・モーツァルト　ポロネーズ集

6つの感傷的なポロネーズOp.17,　4つの感傷的なポロネーズOp.22,　2つのポロネーズOp.26

Edited by Sonoko Maejima

前島園子──校訂・解説

全音楽譜出版社

Preface ●序文

Zum Anlaß der Erstveröffentlichung in Japan

Am 1. Oktober 1841 konstituierte sich unter dem Protektorat des Salzburger Kardinal-Erzbischofs Friedrich IV. Johann Fürst von Schwarzenberg (1809/1836-1850/1885) das Institut "Dom-Musik-Verein und Mozarteum", aus dem 1880 die Internationale Stiftung Mozarteum hervorging.

Constanze Nissen, verwitwete Mozart, die zu dieser Zeit in Salzburg noch lebte — sie starb am 6. März 1842 — hätte es gerne gesehen, daß ihr jüngster Sohn Franz Xaver (1791-1844), künstlerischer Leiter dieser Institution geworden wäre, Es kam aber anders: Alcis Taux (1817-1861), der 1839 als Operndirigent an das k.k. Theater in Salzburg kam, wurde zum Direktor des jungen Vereins gewählt.

Im September 1842, als Mozarts Denkmal in Salzburg enthüllt wurde, reiste Franz Xaver von Wien aus in die Heimatstadt seines Vaters, spielte hier das d-Moll-Klavierkonzert KV 466, schrieb für die Festveranstaltung einen "Fest-Chor" nach Motiven von Kompositionen seines Vaters.

Am 29. Juli 1844 starb Franz Xaver in Karlsbad. In seinem Testament, das er am 17. Juni 1842 verfaßt hatte, bestimmte er, "daß die in seinem Nachlasse befindlichen Manuskripte und eigenhändig geschriebenen musikalischen Fragmente seines großen Vaters, mehrere Familienschriften, das Portrait desselben und mehrere andere Familienportraite, ferner das Klavier, bei welchem der große Mozart in der letzteren Zeit seine hochberühmten Werke komponierte, und seine ganze Bibliothek dem Mozarteum als bleibendes Denkmal seines Vaters ausgefolgt werden sollen".

Über den "Dom-Musik-Verein und Mozarteum" kam die Bibliothek Franz Xavers an die Internationale Stiftung Mozarteum. Sie enthält große musikalische Schatze, auch die kompositionen Franz Xavers. Die hier abgedruckten 12 Polonaisen kommen folglich direkt aus den Händen des jüngsten Mozart-Sohnes. Nicht nur Franz Xaver, sondern auch sein Bruder Carl (1784-1858), der in Mailand verstarb, vermachte seine Bibliothek dem Mozarteum.

In der letzten Zeit ist die Musik Franz Xavers immer wieder in den Blickpunkt der Musikwelt gerückt, werden seine 12 Polonaisen von Kennern und Liebhabern wieder geschätzt und gespielt.

Dr. Friedrich Gehmacher
Präsident
Internationale Stiftung Mozarteum
Salzburg

To The First Edition in Japan

On October 1, 1841, under the protection of Cardinal Archbishop Friedrich IV, Johann Fürst von Schwarzenberg (1809/1836-1850/1885), the institute "Cathedral Music Society and Mozarteum", which later in 1880 developed to International Mozarteum Foundation.

Mozart's widow Constanze Nissen (d March 6, 1842), who then resided in Salzburg, wished and made efforts to secure for her youngest son Franz Xaver a position of the artistic director at this newly founded Institute only in vain, and Alois Taux (1817-1861), who came to Salzburg in 1839 as an opera conductor of Royal Theater, was elected a director.

In September, 1842, Franz Xaver, who visited his father's hometown Salzburg at the occasion of celebration for an unveiling of the Mozart Statue, Played Piano Concerto in D Minor kv466, and composed specially for this celebration "Festive Chorus" based on his father's motif.

On July 29, 1844, Franz Xaver died in Karlsbad. In his testamect dated June 17, 1842, he stated as follows: "My great father's manuscripts and music fragments in his own handwriting, family documents and portraits, and other various portraits of kinship, as well as the piano which the great Mozart used for composing the most important works in his latter days and also all of his private library should be donated to Mozarteum as my father's permanent monument."

Franz Xaver's private library was transferred through "Cathedral Music Society and Mozarteum" to administration of International Mozarteum Foundation. In this musical treasury of private library were included the works by Franz Xaver himself. Accordingly the 12 polonaises presently published are what have been left directly from Mozart's youngest son, Franz Xaver Wolfgang Mozart himself. His brother Carl Thomas (1784-1858), who died in Milan, also left his bibliotheca by will to Mozarteum.

In recent years, Franz Xaver's music often comes into the limelight in the music world, and his twelve polonaises are sought after again by professionals and music lovers.

Dr. Friedrich Gehmacher
President
International Mozarteum Foundation,
Salzburg

日本からの初出版に寄せて

1841年10月1日、ザルツブルグの大司教枢機卿フリードリヒ4世、ヨハン・フュルスト・フォン・シュヴァルツェンベルグ（1809／1836－1850／1885）の保護下に、後の1880年に国際財団モーツァルテウムへと発展した〈大聖堂音楽協会兼モーツァルテウム〉が成立しました。

当時、ザルツブルグ在住であったモーツァルトの未亡人コンスタンツェ・ニッセン（1842年3月6日死去）は末息子、フランツ・クサヴァーをこの協会の芸術監督にせんと願い、運動しましたが、それは実現されず：1839年王室劇場オペラ指揮者として、ザルツブルグに招かれたアロイス・タウクス（1817－1861）が、その地位に就任しました。

1842年9月、モーツァルト像除幕祝典に際し、ウィーンから父の故郷ザルツブルグに着いたフランツ・クサヴァーはニ短調のピアノ協奏曲KV466を演奏し、また、この式典の為に父の作品モティーフによる"祝典合唱"を書き下ろしました。

1844年7月29日、カールス・バートで死去したフランツ・クサヴァーは1842年6月17日付けの遺言状の中に以下の事項を定めました。〈相続財産のうち、偉大な父の原稿や直筆フラグメント、また家族文書や肖像画、その他種々の親族の肖像画、さらに偉大なモーツァルトが晩年、最も有名な作品を作曲する際に、使用したピアノ、またその他所持する全ての蔵書を父の不変の記念碑としてモーツァルテウムに引き渡すべし〉

こうしてフランツ・クサヴァーの蔵書は〈大聖堂音楽協会兼モーツァルテウム〉を経て国際財団モーツァルテウムの維持下に至りました。
この音楽的宝庫とも言うべき蔵書の中には、またフランツ・クサヴァー自身の作品も含まれていました。したがって、ここに出版された12曲のポロネーズはモーツァルトの末息子、フランツ・クサヴァー・ヴォルフガング・モーツァルト自身から直接に託されたものです。

ミラノで世を去った彼の兄、カール・トーマス（1784－1858）もまた彼の蔵書をモーツァルテウムに遺贈しました。
近来、フランツ・クサヴァーの音楽は、たびたび音楽界の視点に置かれ、また12のポロネーズは専門家や愛好家の間で再び求められています。

国際財団モーツァルテウム総裁
Dr. フリードリッヒ・ゲーマッハー

Recommendation ● 推薦文

Der erste Gesamtausgabe der Polonaisen von Franz Xaver Wolfgang Mozart

Franz Xaver Wolfgang Mozart komponierte seine "VI POLONAISES mélancoliques pour le Pianoforte", die 1816 bei Breitkopf & Härtel in Leipzig erschienen, im Jahre 1814. Wegen der Drucklegung kam es mit dem Verlag zu großen Unstimmigkeiten, ja Mozarts Sohn war erbost, wie das renommierte Haus mit ihm umging. Am 29. November 1815 schrieb er seinem Verleger, daß er anderthalb Jahre seine Ungeduld unterdrückt und vergebens seines Polonaisen op.17 im Druck erwartet habe. Er ersuchte Breitkopf & Härtel, den Druck zu beschleunigen, schrieb, "sollten Sie aber Ihren Entschluß, diese Kleinigkeit in Verlag zu nehmen, geändert haben (obwohl ich das warum? nicht begreifen kann) so ersuche ich Sie, mir selbe, so bald möglich, zurücksenden zu wollen". "Kleinigkeit" nannte Franz Xaver Wolfgang also sein Opus 17.

Die Quatre Polonaises mélancoliques op.22 verlegte Peters in Leipzig 1822. Gewidmet sind sie Alexandra Rosalia Rzewuska, geb. Prinzessin Lubowinska (1791-1865).

Franz Xaver Wolfgang Mozart hat seine "Polonaises mélancoliques" sehr geliebt, oft hat er sie in Salons einem begeisterten Publikum vorgespielt.

Die Polonaise de bal und dis Polonaise élégante op.26, die nach 1821 bei piller in Lemberg herausgegeben wurden, sind der Gräfin Glogolvska, geb. Gräfin Stadnicka, dediziert.

1841 wurde Franz Xaver Wolfgang Mozart Ehrenkapellmeister des "Dom-Musik-Verein und Mozarteum". Ein Jahr darauf, am 10. Dezember 1842 ernannte ihn die "Congregazione ed Accademia Santa Cecilia" in Rom zum "Maestro Compositore onorario".
1842 wohnte er mit seinem Bruder Carl Thomas der Feier zur Enthüllung des Mozart-Denkmals bei. Beim Festkonzert spielte er das berühmte d-Moll Klavierkonzert seines Vaters (KV 466) und es war ein großer Erfolg. Dies war sein letzter öffentlicher Auftritt als Pianist. Kurz danach wurde er von einem Magenleiden befallen und ging nach Karlsbad, um es zu heilen, doch verstarb er dort am 29. Juli 1844.

The First Collection of Polonaises by Franz Xaver Wolfgang Mozart Completed

Franz Xaver Mozart Composed "Six Melancholic Polonaises for Piano" in 1814, which was published by Breitkopf & Härtel, Leipzig, in 1816. At the beginning there was a considerable conflict in opinion with the publisher, and naturally the son of Mozart got enraged with the treatment of this renowned publisher. In his letter dated November 29, 1815, he wrote that he had not only been forced to endure for one and half years but vainly anticipated the publication of Polonaises Op.17, and requested Breitkopf & Härtel to hasten the printing, saying "If you have no intention to undertake these little pieces for any reason I do not understand, I would ask you anyway to send them back to me." It was nothing but this collection of short pieces of Op.17 that Franz Xaver Wolfgang called "little pieces".

Four Melancholic Polonaises Op.22 was published in 1822 by Peters in Leipzig. They were dedicated to Alexandra Rosalia Rzewuska, nee Princess Lubowinska, (1791-1865).

Franz Xaver was so satisfied with Melancholic Polonaises, it is said, that he often played them in response to an impressed audience in salons.

Polonaise of Ball Op.26 and Elegant Polonaise are short pieces published by Piller in Lemberg later than 1821. They were dedicated to countess. Glogolvska, nee countess. Stadnicka.

Franz Xaver was appointed Honorary Conductor of "Cathedral Music Society and Mozarteum" in 1841, and further on December 10, 1842, Honorary Composer by "Congregation of Santa Cecilia Academy" in Rome.
He attended with his brother Carl Thomas the unveiling ceremony of Mozart's memorial statue in 1842, and at the memorial music festival, played his father's famous Piano Concerto in D minor, kv466, receiving uproarious applause. This happened to be the last stage performance of himself as a pianist, and he passed away on July 29, 1844, in Karlsbad, where he had visited for recuperation from stomach disorder.

フランツ・クサヴァー・ヴォルフガング・モーツァルト初のポロネーズ全曲集成る

フランツ・クサヴァー・ヴォルフガング・モーツァルトは、1816年にライプツィヒのブライトコップ＆ヘルテル社から出版したピアノ小品集「6つの感傷的ポロネーズ」作品17を1814年に書き下ろした。出版に際し、出版社側とかなり意見の食い違いが生じ、当然のことながらモーツァルトの息子はこの名声ある出版社の扱いに憤った。

彼は1815年11月29日付けの手紙に1年半も我慢した上に、作品17のポロネーズの出版を無駄に期待したと書き、ブライトコップ＆ヘルテル社に印刷を急がせようと以下のように要請したのである。"もし貴殿がこれらのささやかな曲を引き取るおつもりがないのなら（私には何故か？ 理解できぬところですが）、それならそれで早く私宛に返送されるよう願います"
〈ささやかな曲〉とフランツ・クサヴァーが呼んだ小品集が、まさしく作品17である。

4つの感傷的なポロネーズ 作品22は、1822年にライプツィヒのペーター社から出版された。公女ルボウィンスカこと、アレキサンドラ・ロザリア・ルゼウスカ（1791－1865）に献呈されている。感傷的なポロネーズを愛好したフランツ・クサヴァーはサロンなどで感動する聴衆に応えてこれらの曲をしばしば演奏したという。

作品26の舞踏会のポロネーズ並びに優雅なポロネーズは、レンベルクのピラー社から1821年以降に出版された小品で、スタドゥニスカ伯家出のグロゴルスカ伯夫人に献呈されている。

フランツ・クサヴァーは1841年〈大聖堂音楽協会兼モーツァルテウム〉の名誉指揮者に、また1842年12月10日、ローマの〈サンタ・チェチリア・アカデミー協会〉から〈名誉作曲家〉に命名される。1842年、ザルツブルグで催されたモーツァルト記念像除幕式に、兄・カール・トーマスと列席し、その記念音楽祭では父親の有名なニ短調ピアノ協奏曲kv466を演奏し、大喝采を起こす。奇しくもこれがピアニストとして彼の最後の演奏舞台となり、1844年7月29日、胃病のため療養に行ったカールスバートで不帰の客となる。

Prof. Dr. Rudolph Angermüller
Internazionale Stiftung Mozarteum
Salzburg

Prof. Dr. Rudolph Angermüller
International Mozarteum Foundation,
Salzburg

ルドルフ・アンガーミューラー博士
国際財団モーツァルテウム　ザルツブルグ

CONTENTS

Portrait von Franz Xaver Wolfgang Mozart (1791-1844)
肖像画：フランツ・クサヴァー・ヴォルフガング・モーツァルト（1791-1844）

Handschrift des Komponisten "Polonaise mélancolique" op.17-nr.1, datiert 15. April 1814
自筆楽譜「感傷的なポロネーズ」作品17第1番、1814年4月15日付

フランツ・クサヴァー・ヴォルフガング・モーツァルト（1791—1844）

●ポロネーズ集に寄せて

　フランツ・クサヴァー・モーツァルトは父・ヴォルフガング・アマデウス・モーツァルトの余命わずか数ヶ月を残す1791年の夏、7月26日にウィーンで誕生し、幼い頃から父・モーツァルト同様に非凡な音楽的才能を著わし周囲の人々の期待を集めました。

　5歳の頃、プラハ滞在中にまずF. X. ニメチェク（1766—1849）にピアノの手ほどきを受けたフランツ・クサヴァーは当地で神童と噂にのぼりました。再びウィーンに呼び戻された彼は、当時の著名な音楽教師にあずけられ、ピアノをS. ノイコム（1778—1858）、A. シュトライヒャー（1761—1833）、また父、モーツァルトの弟子であったJ. N. フンメル（1778—1837）に学びました。又、一般音楽教育はJ. N. フォーグラー（1749—1814）や、あのベートーヴェンに対位法を教えたJ. G. アルブレヒツベルガー（1736—1809）、そしてA. サリエリ（1750—1825）の研鑽をあおぎました。

　1800年頃、折りしもW. A. モーツァルトの天才性が再び世間で騒がれ始めた時のこと、母・コンスタンツェは感受性豊かなこの末息子、フランツ・クサヴァーに「第二のモーツァルト」を夢見てか、アーティストネームを"W. A. モーツァルト二世"として世に送り出したのです。

　こうして同じ職業分野で偉大な父の名を背負った息子、フランツ・クサヴァーは至る所でその父と比較評価される人生を余儀なくされ、その運命の重さが本来明るい彼の性格に次第に屈折の影をもたらしてゆくのです。

　ウィーンで望みの職を得られず、17歳のフランツ・クサヴァーは当時オーストリア領のレンベルク（現在ロシアのウクライナ地方、ロフ）に行き、そこでポーランド出身のバウロフスキー伯家のピアノ教師をしつつ創作活動に専心、また28歳を迎えた1819年春には足掛け二年のヨーロッパ大演奏旅行を遂行し、若きピアニストとして全盛時代を築きます。

　"感傷的なポロネーズ"は、当時、レンベルクで流行していたM. K. オジンスキー（1765—1833）のポロネーズにヒントを得て作曲された初々しくロマンティックな魅力溢れる小品集で、閃めくパッセージにフランツ・クサヴァーの豊かな情趣と才能がうかがわれます。

感傷的なポロネーズ　作品17

　　　1）ロ短調　2）ホ短調　3）ハ短調

　　　4）ト短調　5）ヘ短調　6）ニ短調

感傷的なポロネーズ　作品22

　　　1）ハ短調　2）イ短調

　　　3）ヘ短調　4）ト短調

2つのポロネーズ　作品26

　　　1）舞踏会のポロネーズ　ニ長調

　　　2）優雅なポロネーズ　ハ長調

　作品17と22は、ポロネーズが全て短調で統一され（中間部トリオのみ長調）感傷的と題された由縁でしょう。三部の古典メヌエット形式とはいうものの初期ロマン派の時代精神が初々しく息づく「抒情ピアノ小曲」となっています。

　またステップで興を起こす左手とそれに乗って優雅に出現する右手の楽想や装飾は、かのショパン（1810—1849）を連想させますが、ちなみに1814年に書きおろされた"感傷的なポロネーズ"作品17がライプチヒで初版された1816年、ショパンはまだ6歳で丁度、ピアノを習い始めた頃でした。作品17のポロネーズ集は、当時大変愛好され、翌1817年には第二版が発行されるほどの人気でした。これらのポロネーズは初期ロマン派時代にさしかかったヨーロッパの大気の中で奇しくも「モーツァルトからショパンへの」ピアノ音楽発展史を織り成しました。

　"感傷的なポロネーズ"は、フランツ・クサヴァー・モーツァルト自身の抒情日記、かの"ヨゼフィーネ"への淡い慕情が秘められた"音の徒然草"といえます。

　楽譜に託された彼の想いが時を経て今、聴く人の胸に美しくメランコリックに甦えることでしょう。

　日本からの初出版を心からよろこぶものです。

　楽譜は初版を底本に、校閲しました。フレージング、強弱記号そしてユニークなペダル記号とも原典どおりです。参考に指使いのみ記入しました。

　最後に資料提供いただいた在・ザルツブルグのモーツァルテウム国際財団に厚く感謝の意を表しますと共に、日本初出版を3年間ご支援下さったルドルフ・アンガーミュラー博士やジュヌヴィエーヴ・ジェフレイ女史をはじめとする同研究室の皆様方にこの紙面をお借りして心からお礼申し上げます。

　　　　　　　　　　　　　ザルツブルグにて　　'96年1月20日

　　　　　　　　　　　　　　　　　　　　　　　前島園子

12 Polonaisen für Klavier
von Franz Xaver Wolfgang Mozart (1791-1844)

Als Franz Xaver Wolfgang Mozart am 26. Juli 1791 in Wien zur Welt kam, waren seinem Vater Wolfgang Amadeus nur mehr wenige Monate zu leben gegönnt.
Er war Mozarts jüngster Sohn und ein eher sensibles Kind. Gleich seinem Vater, versetzte er bereits als Kind seine Umwelt durch sein musikalisches Talent in Erstaunen.

Mit 5 Jahren erhielt er seinen ersten Klavierunterricht bei dem Mozart-Biographen Professor Franz Xaver Niemetschek (1766-1849) in Prag, wo sich bald sein Ruf als Wunderkind zu verbreiten begann. Im Jahr 1798 wurde Franz Xaver von seiner Mutter Constanze nach Wien zurückgeholt.

Obwohl sie mittlerweile in ärmlichen Verhältnissen leben mußte, sorgte sie tatkräftig für seine Ausbildung durch die damals renommiertesten Lehrer.
So konnte Franz Xaver sein Musikstudium bei Sigismund Neukomm (1778-1858), Andreas Streicher (1761-1833), Johann Nepomuk Hummel (1778-1837), Georg Joseph Vogler (1749-1814), Johann Georg Albrechtsberger (1736-1809) und Antonio Salieri (1750-1825) fortsetzen.
Seine erste Eigenkomposition, ein Klavierquartett, schuf er mit 11 Jahren. Es ist ebenso, wie das seines Vaters, in "g- Moll" gehalten und zeigt zugleich die jugendlichen Ambitionen Franz Xavers,

Zu dieser Zeit, nämlich um 1800, wurde auch die Genialität W. A. Mozarts von einer breiten Öffentlichkeit wiederentdeckt. Mutter Constanze gab Franz Xaver den Künstlernamen "Wolfgang Amadeus Mozart Sohn", da sie davon träumte, daß aus ihm ein "Zweiter Mozart" werden würde. Damit wurde aber auch das Schicksal des Sohnes vorgezeichnet, der sich nunmehr mit seinem übermächtigen Vater, noch dazu im selben Metier, auseinandersetzen mußte. Dieser Konflikt warf zunehmend einen melancholischen Schatten auf das ansonsten natürlich heitere Gemüt Franz Xavers.

Nachdem er in Wien keine Anstellung finden konnte, nahm er als Siebzehnjähriger bei dem polnischen Grafen Viktor Baworowski eine Stelle als Pianist und Musikerzieher im damaligen österreichischen Lemberg, dem heutigen ukrainischen Lvov, an.

Im Alter von 28 Jahren unternahm er 1819 eine 2-jährige Konzerttournee durch weite Teile Europas, u.a. Rußland, Polen, deutsche und österreichische Länder, die Schweiz, Italien und Dänemark, wobei er als Pianist seine Blütezeit erlebte.
Viele seiner Kompositionen hat er während seiner Lembergerzeit, die bis 1825 andauerte, niedergeschrieben.
Darunter auch die folgenden 12 Polonaisen :

Six Polonaises mélancoliques Op.17

> Nr.1 h-Moll, Nr.2 e-Moll, Nr.3 c-Moll,
> Nr.4 g-Moll, Nr.5 f-Moll, Nr.6 d-Moll,

Quatre Polonaises mélancoliques Op.22

> Nr.1 c-Moll, Nr.2 a-Moll,
> Nr.3 f-Moll, Nr.4 g-Moll

Deux Polonaises Op.26

> Polonaise de Bal, D-Dur
> Polonaise élégante, C-Dur

In sämtlichen in diesem Heft abgedruckten Werken atmet sowohl der gemütvolle Charakter Franz Xavers als auch der leidende früh-romantische Zeitgeist.
Franz Xaver Knüpft mit diesen Polonaisen an die Polonaisen des Grafen Michael Kleophas Oginski (1765-1833), den er in Lemberg kennengelernt haben dürfte.

Die Polonaises mélancoliques Op.17 wie auch Op.22 sind alle, in Moll geschrieben, lediglich ihr Mittelteil ist jeweils in Dur. Obwohl in der klassischen Form des dreiteiligen Menuetts gehalten, bringt Franz Xaver mit diesen Stücken bereits eine Vorahnung auf die lyrisch-romantischen Klavier-werke, so wie auch die Fiorituren auf chopinische Klaviermusik, Melancholische Polonaisen Op.17 hat Franz Xaver Mozart jedoch bereits im Frühjahr 1812 komponiert-als sie im Jahr 1816 in Leipzig erstmalig gedruckt wurden, war Frédéric Chopin (1810-1849) gerade 6 Jahre alt und begann soeben mit dem Erlernen des Klavierspiels. Die Polonaisen Op.17 waren sehr beliebt, so daß 1817 bereits eine 2. Auflage herausgegeben wurde.
In ihrer Melancholie und eleganten Art, das Klavier einzusetzen, sind diese Kompositionen ein unbekannt gebliebenes Bindeglied der Klaviermusik zwischen Mozart und Chopin.
Die "Polonaises mélancoliques" sind Franz Xavers eigenes lyrisches Tagebuch. Leidend in einer anmutigen, schmeichelnden Art, scheint er vielleicht jene "Josephine" im damaligen Lemberg ansprechen zu wollen.

Ich freue mich, daß durch die vorliegende Erstveröffentlichung dieser 12 Polonaisen in Japan ein musikalisches Vermächtnis des Pianisten und Komponisten Franz Xaver Mozart einer breiten Öffentlichkeit zugänglich gemacht wird.

Die Phrasierung, dynamischen Zeichen sowie auch die überaus interessanten Pedalzeichen wurden originalgetreu dem Erstdruck entnommen. Lediglich die Fingersätze habe ich selbst hinzugefügt.

Abschließend möchte ich der Internationalen Stiftung Mozarteum Salzburg für die Bereitstellung der Originaldrucke, allen voran Herrn Prof. Dr. Rudolph Angermüller und Frau Geneviève Geffray meinen herzlichsten Dank aussprechen.

> Salzburg, den 20. Jänner 1996
> Sonoko Maejima

12 POLONAISES FOR PIANO

by Franz Xaver Wolfgang Mozart (1791-1844)

Franz Xaver Wolfgang Mozart was born in Vienna on July 26, in the summer of 1791, when his father Wolfgang Amadeus had but few months left to live.
From an early age Franz Xaver displayed extraordinary musical abilities just like his father and great hopes were entertained of him among the people around.

At the age of five, while ataying in Prague, Franz Xaver learned the rudiments of piano first if all under the tutorship of Franz Xaver Niemetschek (1766-1849) and became the talk of town as an infant prodigy. Then he was called back to Vienna and committed to the care of a noted music teacher to take piano lessons from Sigismund Neukomm (1778-1858), Andreas Streicher (1761-1833) and also Johann Nepomuk Hummel (1778-1837), who had been a pupil of his father Mozart. He further prosecuted his studies in general music education under Georg Joseph Vogler (1749-1814), Johann Georg Albrechtsberger (1736-1809), who gave lessons in counterpoint to that Beethoven, and Antonio Salieri (1750-1825).

Around the year of 1800, when it happened that a transcendent genius of Wolfang Amadeus Mozart again began to make a stir, Constanze sent out her susceptible youngest son Franz Xaver to the world under the artist name of "Wolfgang Amadeus Mozart son", presumably dreaming of "The Second Mozart".

Thus Franz Xaver, a son burdened with the great name of his father in the same field of profession, was obliged to be involved in the life where he was compared and estimated in the light of his father wherever he went, and his originally light-hearted disposition gradually grew shadowed with warp under such a heavy load of destiny.

Franz Xaver, 17 years old, unable to obtain a desired situation in Vienna, went to Lemberg of Austrian dominion at that time (present Lvov in Ukrainian district of Russia), where he devoted himself to creative activity while engaged as a pisno teacher at Count Viktor Bawrowski's family of Polish origin.

Attaining his 28th year in the spring of 1819, he started for a grand concert tour in Europe which extended pver two calendar years, and established his prime as a young pianist.

"Melancholic Polonaises", composed after the idea of a Polonaise by Michael Kleophas Oginski (1765-1833) then prevailing in Lemberg, is a collection of short pieces full of gracefulness, and in their brilliant passages are found affluent sentiment and telent of Franz Xaver.

Six Polonaises mélancoliques, Op.17

No.1 H Minor, No.2 E Minor, No.3 C Minor
No.4 G Minor, No.5 F Minor, No.6 D Minor

Quatre Polonaises mélancoliques, Op.22

No.1 C Minor, No.2 A Minor
No.3 F Minor, No.4 G Minor

Deux Polonaises, Op.26

Polonaise de Bal, D Major
Polonaise élégante, C Major

All the Polonaises in Op.17 and 22 are unified by a minor key (except the major at the trio part), which probably is the reason why they were entitled "Melancholic". Even in its classical minuet style of three parts, they turned out to be "lyrical short pieces for piano" where the spirit of the times of early romantic school is naively breathing.

The interest enliven by the left hand at the step, and the motif and ornaments of the right hand which elegantly appear along with it, remind us of that Chopin. Incidentally, when the first edition of Six Melancholic Polonaises, Op.17 composed in 1814, was published in 1816 in Leipzig, Chopin was still six years old and just started to take piano lessons. The Polonaises of Op.17 became great favorites of those days and was so popular that the second edition was published in the next year 1817. These Polonaises coincidentally woven up a developing history of piano music "from Mozart to Chopin" in the atmosphere of Enrope where the romanticism was approaching.

"Melancholic Polonaises" were a lyrical diary of Franz Xaver Mozart himself, or "Moments musicaux" secreting his faint affection to that "Josephine". His longing entrusted to the music, even after so long a time, will be brought back to life beautifully and melancholically in the mind of those who listen to it.

I am very pleased with publication of the first edition of this music in Japan. For this publication, the original first edition was used, representing the phrasing, the dynamics and the unique pedalling of the original faithfully. Only the fingering is added for reference.

I would like to express my sincere gratitude to International Mozarteum Foundation, Salzburg, who supplied me with precious materials, and also my hearty thanks to Prof. Dr. Rudolph Angermüller and Madame Geneviève Geffray who extended their support for the Japanese first edition over three years, and also to all of their staffs as well.

Salzburg, January 20, 1996
Sonoko Maejima

No. 1

Polonaise op. 17

F. X. Mozart
(1791—1844)

Fine

Trio

legato

Polonaise da capo

No. 2

Polonaise op. 17

F. X. Mozart
(1791—1844)

Trio

Polonaise da capo

No. 3

Polonaise op. 17

F. X. Mozart
(1791 — 1844)

Tempo di ballo

Fine

Trio

dolce

Polonaise da capo

No. 4

Polonaise op. 17

F. X. Mozart
(1791—1844)

Allegretto moderato

Polonaise da capo

No. 5

Polonaise op. 17

F. X. Mozart
(1791—1844)

Polonaise da capo

No. 6

Polonaise op. 17

F. X. Mozart
(1791—1844)

No. 1

Polonaise op. 22

F. X. Mozart
(1791—1844)

Risoluto

Fine

Trio

Fine

Trio da capo al Fine e poi Polonaise

No. 2

Polonaise op. 22

F. X. Mozart
(1791—1844)

Andantino con moto

Dal Segno sin' al Fine

Trio

Dal Segno sin' al Fine e poi Polonaise

No. 3

Polonaise op. 22

F. X. Mozart
(1791–1844)

Allegretto moderato

scen - - do   f   fp   pp

Dal Segno

Trio   p

Ped.

Fine

cre - scen - do   fp   a tempo

ritard.

Trio D.S. e poi Polonaise sin' al Fine

No. 4

Polonaise op. 22

F. X. Mozart
(1791—1844)

Andante espressivo

*) 2. time, 2回目

Polonaise da capo sin' al Fine

Polonaise de Bal op. 26

F. X. Mozart
(1791—1844)

Fine

Polonaise da capo sin' al Fine

Polonaise élégante op. 26

F. X. Mozart
(1791—1844)

Trio

Fine

Trio da capo sin' al Fine e poi Polonaise

■ Editor: Sonoko Maejima (pianist)

After finishing her studies at the TOHO-GAKUEN School of Music in Tokyo, Sonoko Maejima came to Europe and continued to study piano with Prof. Kurt Neumüller at the Mozarteum Salzburg, where she received her Diploma as concert pianist with honours and in addition was awarded the Lili-Lehmann medal — the highest distinction for a musician that the Mozarteum can bestow.

She pursued her studies of piano with Prof. Alberto Mozzati in Milano and chamber music with Maestro Antonio Janigro and Sándor Végh.

Sonoko Maejima has performed solo recitals and several chamber music engagements in Germany, Spain, Italy regularly in Austria and Japan, She played piano concertos with Tokyo Symphony Orchestra, Mexico Symphony Orchestra and Mozarteum Orchestra at big festival hall in Salzburg.

Sonoko Maejima holds teaching post at the Mozarteum Salzburg where she now lives and has been also a guest professor at Tokyo College of Music since 1992.

■ 前島園子プロフィール

　4才よりピアノを始め岡林千枝子、井口愛子、井口基成、斉藤秀雄氏のもとで研鑽を積む。桐朋学園大学音楽学部ピアノ科を首席卒業後、オーストリア政府より奨学金を得て、ザルツブルグのモーツァルテウム音楽大学でクルト・ノイミュラー教授に師事、在学中からチャイコフスキーやリストなどのピアノ協奏曲を演奏し、活躍をはじめる。

　1973年同大学を最優秀首席で卒業。国際財団モーツァルテウムよりリリー・レイマンメダルを授与される。

　その後、イタリアのミラノでアルベルト・モツァーティ教授に師事する他、室内楽をマエストロ・アントニオ・ヤニグロ並びにシャンドール・ヴェーク両氏に学び、音楽的芸術的に多大な影響を受ける。ザルツブルグに在住し、オーストリアを中心にドイツ、イタリア、スペイン、日本でリサイタルや、数々の室内楽アンサンブルを共演。ソリストとして東京交響楽団やメキシコ・シンフォニー・オーケストラに招かれ、またザルツブルグの祝祭大劇場では、モーツァルテウム・オーケストラとショパンのピアノ協奏曲を協演する。

　現在モーツァルテウム音楽大学で後進の指導にあたる傍ら、同時に、東京音楽大学のゲスト教授を務める。

クサヴァー・モーツァルト
感傷的なポロネーズ

父モーツァルトの溢れる才能を受け継いだ甘美で美しい12のポロネーズ
CD VICC-178 ●前島 園子 (ピアノ)

Victor　JVC　Victor Entertainment, Inc.

フランツ・クサヴァー・モーツァルト
ポロネーズ集　　　　　　　　　　　　　　●

校訂・解説 ——————————————— 前島園子
第1版第1刷発行 ——————————————— 1996年1月20日
第1版第3刷発行 ——————————————— 2011年5月31日
発行 ——————————————— 株式会社全音楽譜出版社
——————————————— 東京都新宿区上落合2丁目13番3号〒161-0034
——————————————— TEL・営業部03・3269-0121
——————————————— 出版部03・3267-4321
——————————————— ISBN978-4-11-106900-2

1105016